This book belongs to

For Iris & Freya

For permission requests, write to the publisher at:
hello@antheadesignstudio.com

Title: Ollie Tries a New Sport
ISBN: 978-93-344-2187-3
First edition, 2025

Summary

Ollie is a self-conscious octopus who has a hard time trying her hand at new things. When sea basketball starts, she wants to join in but is worried of embarrassing herself. She later learns that her strength lies in her uniqueness and that there are friends who accept her for who she is.

OLLIE TRIES A NEW SPORT

Written and Illustrated by
Priyadarshini Das Sharma

Down in the sea where the kelp forests sway,
Ollie the Octopus dreamed of a day…

…she'd join in the games everyone played.
But trying new things made Ollie afraid.

Sea basketball was starting,
the teams were made of critters so fast,

Ollie felt clumsy, and was certain she'd come in last.

What if I tumble?

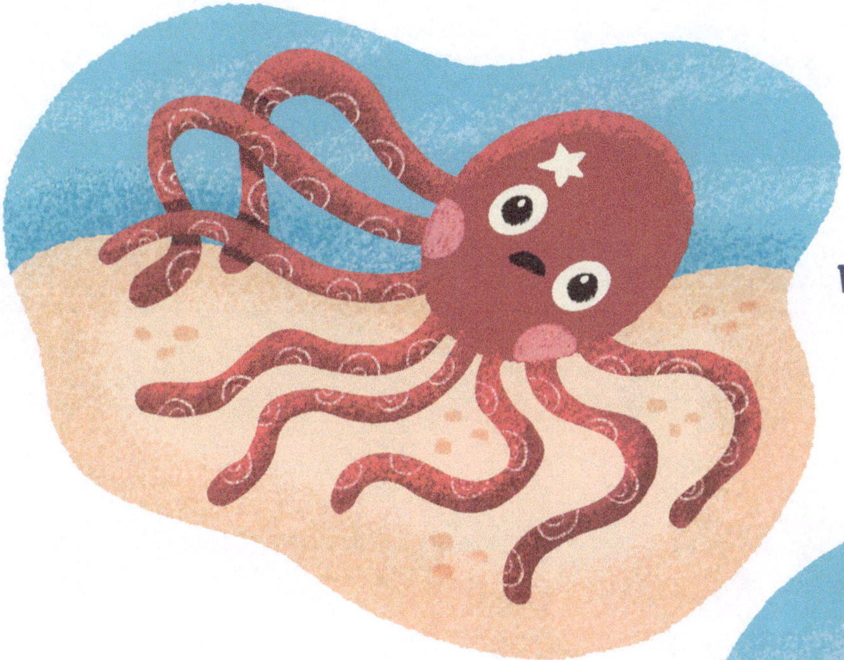

What if I fall?

What if my arms get
stuck on the ball?

"Come, join us", called out
Coral, a bright, zippy fish.

"It's meant to be fun, not perfect.
Just give it a swish!"

Ollie swam closer, her heart full of doubt,
"Eight arms are too many, I'll surely stand out!"

The hermit crab blew his whistle,
but Ollie froze in place,

While the dolphins zipped forward in
a lightning fast chase.

Ollie fumbled, tumbled and tripped
on the sand,

She wished she could hide
inside a shell close at hand

Then, suddenly, the ball bounced her way,

Could Ollie be brave and join in the play?

She reached with one arm,
then another, then more…

…eight arms made her nimble,
like never before!

She dribbled, juggled, and spun with flair,
The crowd gave a cheer that rang through the air.

Ollie felt lighter, her worries grew small,

"My arms are my superpower, not a problem at all!"

Everyone applauded, they shouted her name,
Ollie the Octopus had turned the whole game!

GO
OLLIE!

Now, whenever she's scared of
trying something new,

Ollie tells herself, "Remember what eight arms can do."

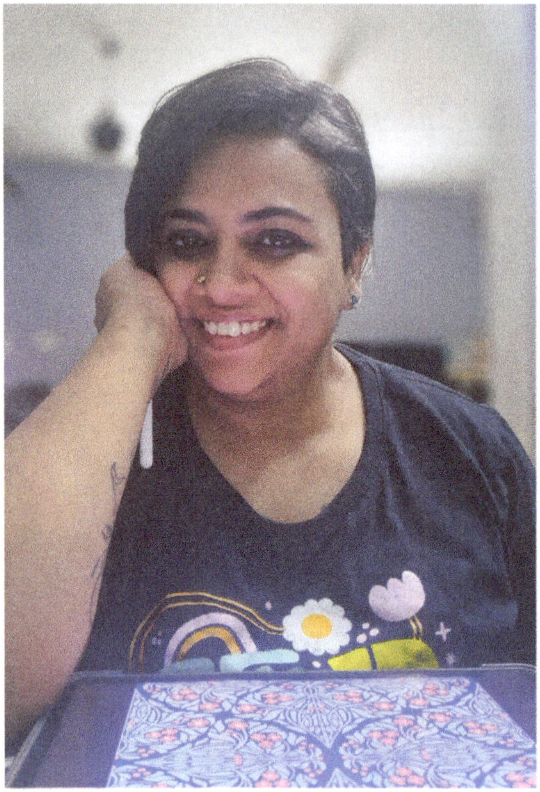

Priyadarshini is an illustrator and storyteller who loves creating tales filled with color, kindness, and courage. When not dreaming up adventures for talking animals, she can usually be found sketching, reading, or enjoying time with her daughters and six dogs. Ollie Tries a New Sport is her debut picture book.

9 789334 421873

Printed at Repro India Ltd.